Powerful Pearls of Wisdom, Idioms, Meditations and Poignant Proverbs to Live By

Terri L. McCrea, M.Ed., LPC

Powerful Pearls of Wisdom, Idioms, Meditations, Idioms and Poignant Proverbs to Live By

All rights reserved. Unless otherwise noted, no part of this book may be reproduced in any form, except brief reviews, without written permission of the publisher.

Cassaundra Mulligan, Editor

Cover and interior arrangements by –
Kathrine Rend – Rend Graphics
www.rendgraphics.com

Printed in the United States of America.
ISBN 978-1-7355737-8-6

Poetic Expressions by Terri
Terri L. McCrea, M.Ed., LPC, LPC/S
1643 B Savannah Highway, #113
Charleston, SC 29407
Mobile (843) 437-7572
Fax (843) 763-7202
poeticexpressions@att.net

Powerful Pearls of Wisdom, Idioms, Meditations and Poignant Proverbs to Live By

Dedication

This book is dedicated for those that live in the moment, who aren't afraid to try something new, who wish upon stars, who are transcended through the sounds of the ocean, who cloud watch, who face challenges head on, who are infinite dreamers, who get lost in love struck eyes, who can't wait for each dawn and who can see the best in souls.

Introduction

This empowerment book is filled to the brim with mantras, idioms, meditations and proverbs that will hopefully shift one into a higher mental, physical and spiritual transformational state inspiring one's soul.

Trust your journey.

*You may know
how to fly,
but life
will teach you
how to soar.*

*Open conscious
higher thinking conversations
grows one's soul.*

*Be that
which you desire.*

*Maintain
focus in order
to stay on your
destiny's course.*

*You were not born
to be the object of
someone's projection
or transference.*

*Believe
in your destination.*

*Deprogram
toxic lies,
to not only
live in peace,
but more importantly,
to live free.*

*Don't allow
fear or the unknown
to stop you
from walking
in your purpose.*

*Don't allow guilt or shame
to stop you from speaking
your truths.*

*You learn
as you learn.*

*Don't block
your blessings.*

*The best investment
is in you.*

When lost in translation
about life,
know that
what truly matters
is not your beginning,
but the amazing chapters in
between
and it's
beautiful ending.

Live by...
I will,
I am
and
I can.

*Turn your pain
into a
timeless passion that impacts
mankind.*

*Only invite those into your life
whose capabilities
meet your needs.*

*Allow
your higher self
to direct
your metamorphosis.*

Disloyal, Denigrating, Derogatory, Domineering, Dishonest, Discounting, Disavowing, Degrading, Dismissive, Deceitful and Demeaning behaviors has no place in an Emotionally Available, Authentic and Accountable Relationship.

*One doesn't know
one's strength
until one tries.*

*Leave a
path of glitter
wherever you go.*

*Value each
and every breath.*

*Your actions
in the spotlight
are just as important as your
actions
out of the spotlight.*

*Mindfully
move,
think and
feel in order to be
authentically real.*

*Bloom
from the rain.*

*Honor,
not money,
makes a man.*

*Don't allow
your wants to
cost you
your peace,
your freedom,
your life or
your dreams.*

*Time in silence
will force you
to look within.*

*Life isn't life without
moving songs,
beautiful sunsets
and
a peaceful heart.*

*Breathe
in goodness,
serenity
and love.*

*Never turn your back
to an owl.*

*Live introspectively
in order to
challenge
life's illusions.*

*Allow your
passionate heart
to inspire
your next move.*

*Stop living in the past and
grieving your
joy away.*

Know that you are an original.

The rear view mirror
is small for
a reason.

*Mindful steps
are key to
intentional living.*

Glow.

*Always
protect and balance
your energy.*

*If you survived
from that
twinkle in your
parents eyes,
then fly.*

*Be not only
someone's blessing,
but more importantly,
be someone's
saving grace.*

*Voices are meant
to be heard,
to motivate,
to transform
and
to inspire.*

*Live through soft, yet
iridescent eyes.*

*Know that
it's okay to
be uniquely you.*

Allow hope to prevail over darkness.

Inner beauty radiates through and through.

*Holding on
to the pain
from one's past, will only
maintain one's brokenness
and thwart
one's healing.*

Never be too proud to apologize.

*Be that
unstoppable change maker.*

*When all you have
are paint brushes,
paint.*

*Possess
a
pure and
humble heart.*

*When surrounded by
greatness,
be a sponge.*

*An inconvenience, mishap or setback
can be a blessing
in disguise.*

*Embody the
aura of
a gentle loon.*

*When you have
a dream,
chase it.*

Be an impetus for yearning wings.

Be a rainbow.

*Wherever you live,
make it into a home.*

*Make every step
along your
journey matter.*

*When the universe answers
your prayers,
say thank you.*

*If you have an
older sibling,
remind them
that they
were once young.*

*Live as a
free-spirited
beautiful butterfly.*

*If you have
a younger sibling,
tell them of your life
experiences,
so they won't make the same
mistakes.*

*A brain
is to be challenged.*

*Cut down
all burdening trees
in order to be
an olive bridge.*

*Be that soul
whose eyes
can dream.*

*A brain is a capsule
to be filled with
wells of knowledge.*

*Noses were created
to smell
nature's
fragrant roses, hydrangeas,
gardenias and
lavender buds.*

*Save your soul
from life's clutches
in order to
walk in one's purpose.*

Think higher.

Dream bigger.

*Closed minds
can't bloom.*

*Place your crutches
in a crimson
fire pit
in order
to soar.*

*Gifts are not
to be wasted.*

*Children were born to teach
parents
how to
patiently love.*

*Without ears,
one cannot
experience
the true essence
of the Universe.*

*Souls
were created to
empower souls.*

*Life creates unique
and inspiring stories.*

*Legs
were created
to climb
revered mountains.*

*Treasure
what's right
in front of
your nose,
your eyes
and
your face.*

*Make sure
your living
is not in vain.*

*Legs
were created to
hurdle over
life's obstacles.*

*Hands
were created to
open doors
to one's future.*

*Gracefully
grow young.*

*Eternalize
butterfly love.*

*Refine
through prayer.*

*Be that
luminous star.*

*Hands
were made
to create
moving masterpieces
and captivating
works of art.*

*Take the time to escape
into the beautiful world
of art, music, poetry
and dance.*

*Eyes
were created
to peer into souls
and them
into yours.*

Live, not exist.

*Look beyond
the color
of another's skin.*

*Eyes of
intention shine.*

Keep growing.

*Be that vessel
to remind the free
that they are free.*

*Never allow rain clouds to
extinguish
your fire.*

Fearlessly spread your wings and fly.

*Only date or marry someone
who is capable of nurturing,
feeding
and
healing
your soul.*

*Feet were created
to ground
one's soul.*

*Reclaim your
personal power.*

*Feet were created to run into
the bough
of one's destiny.*

*Don't take
your parents
love,
kindness or presence
for granted.*

*Arms were created
to embrace
the ones we love.*

*Cultivate
your dreams.*

*Stars were created
to shine brightly
amidst the seasons.*

Flowers were created to be plucked.

Be your own advocate.

*It's not
one's height
but one's character.*

*Place your fears
on the
wings of doves.*

*A true friend
walks with you
through
the storm.*

Pure love flourishes.

Honor the living.

*Love
through
Déjà vu eyes.*

Desire

As you journey through this thing called life, create inspiring words of wisdom, idioms, meditations and proverbs that move you to live a life of intention and desire.

Desire to feed, nurture and soothe one's soul with mindful and restorative calming breaths.

Desire to cleanse, free and save self by speaking ugly truths.

Desire to free one's soul from blinding lies and haunting whispers of invaluableness.

Desire to put in the work to strengthen one's fragile and battled mental, physical and spiritual core.

*Desire to reclaim
one's stolen innocence,
one's stolen dignity,
one's stolen name,
and one's stolen worthiness.*

Desire to mend bandaged wounds and harbored cracks.

Desire to give oneself permission to unblock imbalances from the soles of one's feet to the crown of one's head.

Desire to feel, do and be your absolute best.

Desire.

Author

Terri McCrea is a native of Charleston, South Carolina. She has provided counseling for the past 31 years (23 years of that in private practice). She graduated from St. Andrews Parish High School and the College of Charleston before receiving her Master's Degree in Clinical Counseling from The Citadel. She is an Adjunct Professor, a Licensed Addiction Counselor, a Licensed Professional Counselor, a Licensed Professional Counselor Supervisor and served as a Continuing Education provider for the South Carolina Board for Licensed Professional Counselors, Social Workers, Marital and Family Therapists, Psychologists and Psycho-educational Specialists. She conducts local and national workshops on her 20 books as well as a Life Skills Summer Camp (ages five to eighteen), parenting classes, domestic violence classes and anger management classes. She is the Outreach Coordinator of the Old Bethel United Methodist Church's Community Outreach Program. This platform provides preventative, educational, rehabilitative, counseling, and evangelistic services to the Low Country's at-risk youths, families (including the elderly, poor, imprisoned, homeless, disabled and indigent).

Terri writes mental health articles for local magazines and newspapers. She guest appears for mental health segments on local radio and television networks. She can be described as a coach, counselor, visionary, poet, free spirit and believer that everyone and everything has a purpose. She is a member of the Poetry Society of South Carolina (PSSC), the International African American Museum, Old Bethel United Methodist Choir, Gamma Xi Omega Chapter of Alpha Kappa Alpha Sorority, Inc. and is a proud aunt and grand aunt.

Terri is available for book signings, charity events, public/motivational speaking engagements, workshop facilitation, interviews, and expert appearances (radio, web, television and podcast) and poetry readings. She has self-published six self-help guidebooks, four inspirational guides for couples in love, four empowering guides for tots/tweens/teens, a book of wedding vows (English/Spanish translation), a mantra, proverbs and intentions book, a how-to-date book and her first collection of poems (2007-2020).

Terri L. McCrea, M.Ed., LAC, LPC, LPC/S
1643-B Savannah Hwy, Suite 113,
Charleston, SC 29407
(main / principal) 843.437.7572
(facsimile / fax) 843.763.7202
poeticexpressions@att.net

*Visit/ visita:www.btol.com
www.Amazon.com
www.Alibris.com
www.Abebooks.com

Terri L. McCrea's Books

- *The Power of Forgiveness: A Step by Step Guide on How to Let Go, Move On and Begin Living*
- *A Teacher's Dream: A Goal Setting Guide for Tots and Tweens*
- *Problem Solving One on One: Proactive Tactics for Millennium Youths*
- *The Joy of Living: Manifesting a Passionate, Purposeful and Positive You*
- *When You Fly: The Quintessential Guide for Becoming a Present, Centered and Proper Parent*
- *When You Fly: The Quintessential Guide for Becoming a Mentally, Physically, Spiritually and Authentically Aligned Person*
- *When You Fly: The Quintessential Guidebook on How to Become an Emotionally Available, Authentic and Accountable Partnership*
- *When You Fly: The Quintessential Guide for Becoming a Well-Balanced, Well-Aware and Well-Rounded Pupil*
- *I Will Be…(Inspirational Quotes from Men of Honor, In Love and Walking in their Purpose)*
- *I Will Be…(Inspirational Quotes from Women of Faith, in Love and Standing in their Worth)*
- *It's Ok for Boys to…*
- *It's Ok for Girls to…*
- *Intentions*
- *The Book of Mantras: 100 Affirmations to Reframe your Thoughts and Retrain your Brain*
- *Walk Like a King: 100 Virtues of a True Gentleman*
- *Elite Girls Wear Pearls: 100 Virtues of Strong, Empowered and Balanced Women*
- *Powerful Pearls of Wisdom, Meditations, Idioms and Poignant Proverbs to Live By*
- *Soul Encounters: The Collective Poetry of Terri L. McCrea (2007-2020)*
- *Walking in Love: Wedding Vows for that Special Day*
- *2003. 2004, 2nd Edition 2008, What Price Are You Willing to Pay for Love? (Author house: ISBN: 1-418-6299-3 (e-book)/ISBN: 1-4184-3315-2 (Paperback)*

www.ingramcontent.com/pod-product-compliance
Lightning Source LLC
LaVergne TN
LVHW051504070426
835507LV00022B/2906